Ocean Seasons

By Ron Hirschi
Illustrated by Kirsten Carlson

For Jodi, a true miracle—RH

For those who would like to fathom
the depths of nature—KC

Spring is a burst of color on land and in the sea as plants spread their soft, new growth.

Urchins munch on kelp in shallow Pacific waters.
But hungry sea otters eat their share of the urchins,
helping the plants grow into an undersea
forest of many colors.

Many fish, crabs, and shrimp hide and feast in the kelp forest.
Diving birds and swimming seals dine on the young
fish that live in the dense tangles of kelp.

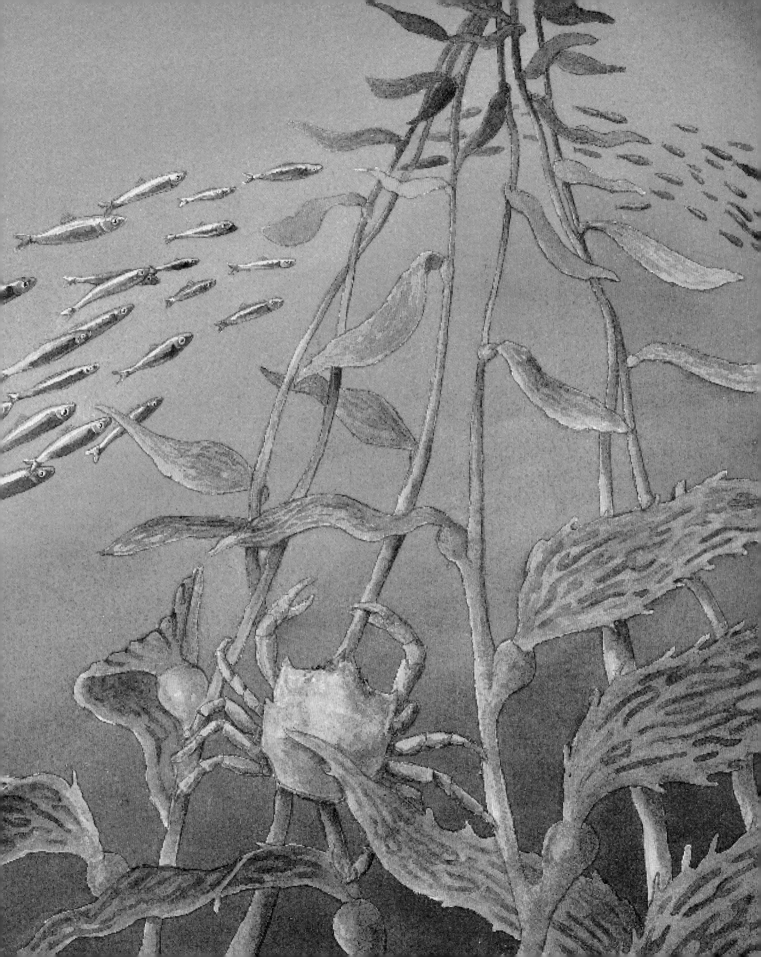

The humpback whales dive and circle under schools of fish.
Looking up, they blow bubbles
that form a net to trap their helpless prey.

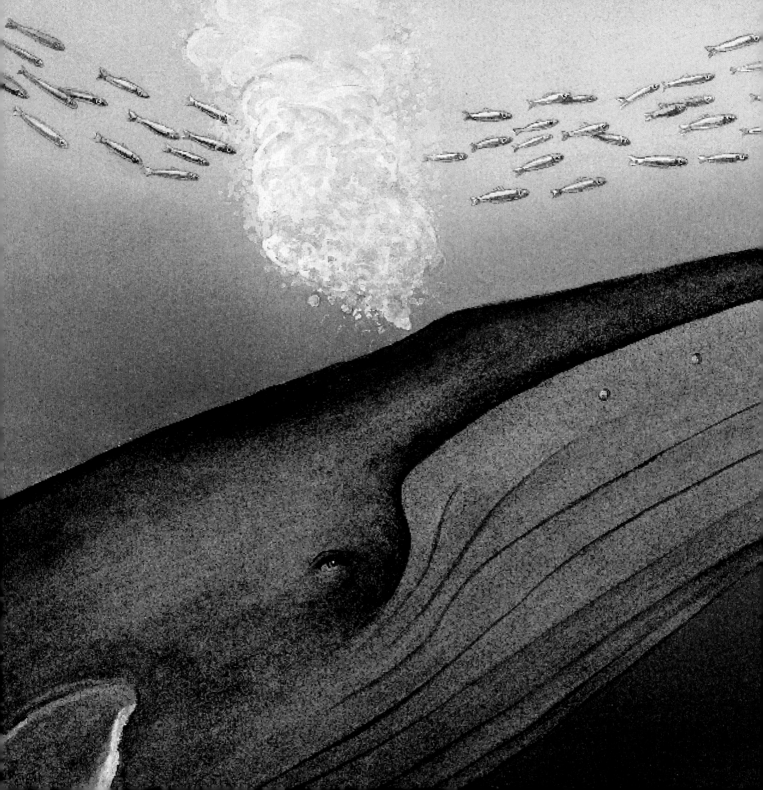

Summer is a calm, blue sea.
Seals sleep in the warm sun.
Baby puffins hatch in burrows on a rocky island.

Fish grow bigger and stronger through the summer; but they are
still food for many birds, bigger fish, and the humpback whales.
Mouths open wide, the whales lunge to the surface,
straining the water to trap fish using the comb-like baleen
that lines their huge mouths.
The whales put on layers of fat as they feast.

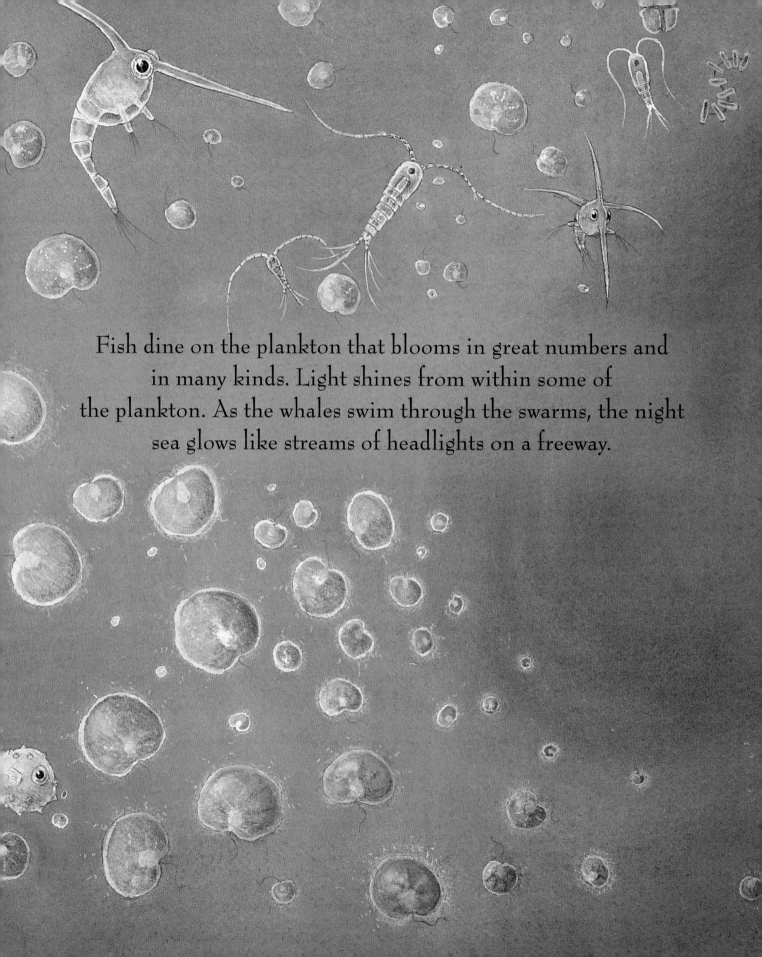

Fish dine on the plankton that blooms in great numbers and
in many kinds. Light shines from within some of
the plankton. As the whales swim through the swarms, the night
sea glows like streams of headlights on a freeway.

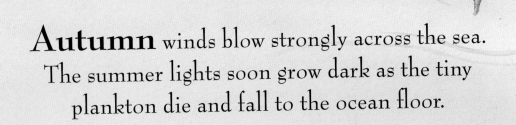

Autumn winds blow strongly across the sea. The summer lights soon grow dark as the tiny plankton die and fall to the ocean floor.

Fall is a time of change on the ocean.
Salmon feed in the kelp forests as they return
to rivers from distant ocean waters.
Seals, sea lions, and humans hunt the salmon.

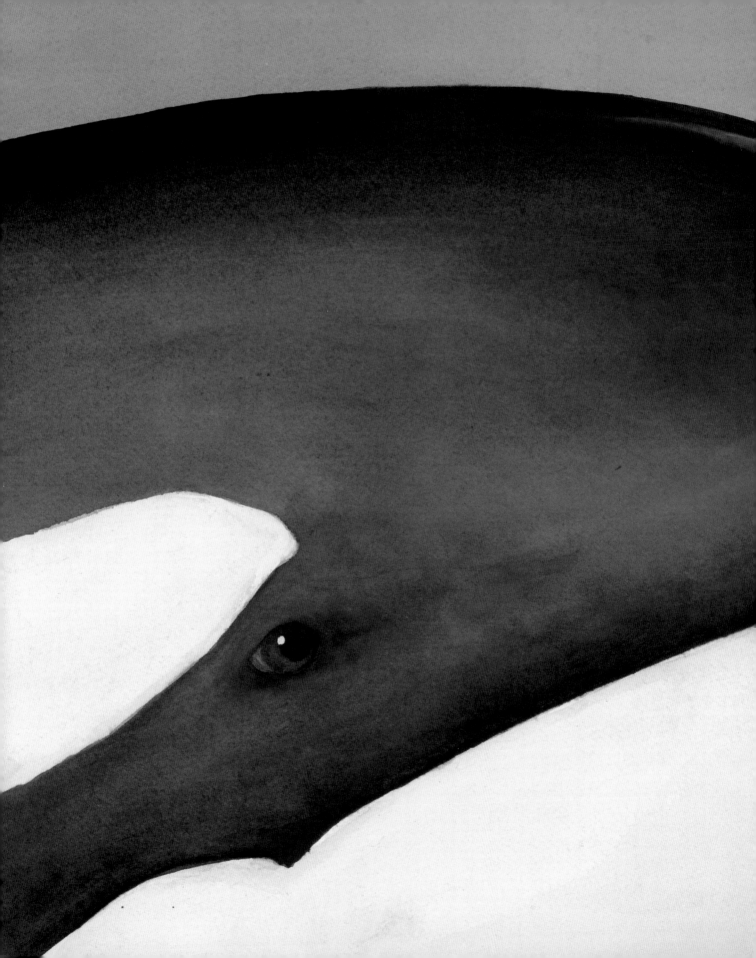

Some orca whales hunt the salmon too.
Other orcas hunt seals,
sea lions, and even humpback whales.

As the **winter** seas grow colder and colder, northern waters become quiet and clear. Atlantic and Pacific humpback whales turn south as icy winds blow.

Winter whales leap and sing in the southern waters.
Just like baby chicks hatch on land in the spring, baby whales
are born in this warm ocean during the tropical winter.

When winter turns to spring, the whales
return to their northern waters as sea plants
begin to spread their sparkling growth once again.

For Creative Minds

Food Web Cards

Cut copies into food web cards. Using the information in the book and on the card, stack each "**predator**" card on top of its "**prey**" card (predators eat the prey). How many cards can you get in one pile? Are there some animals that are always at the top of your pile or on top of the food chain?

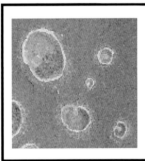

Phytoplankton

Prey: gets its energy from the sun (bottom card)

Predators: small fish, crabs, shrimp, and zooplankton

Phytoplankton

Prey: gets its energy from the sun (bottom card)

Predators: small fish, crabs, shrimp, and zooplankton

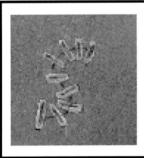

Phytoplankton

Prey: gets its energy from the sun (bottom card)

Predators: small fish, crabs, shrimp, and zooplankton

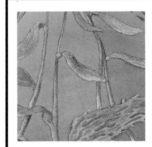

Kelp

Prey: gets its energy from the sun (bottom card)

Predators: urchins, snails, and crabs

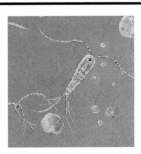

Zooplankton

Prey: phytoplankton and other zooplankton

Predators: small fish, crabs, shrimp, and baleen whales

Urchins

Prey: kelp

Predators: sea otters, fish, crabs, and snails

Sea Otters

Prey: urchins, abalone, crabs, clams, octopuses, fish, and sea stars

Predators: orca whales, bald eagles, and sharks

Small Fish

Prey: phytoplankton, zooplankton, and other small fish

Predators: big fish, crabs, and orca and humpback whales

Small Fish

Prey: phytoplankton, zooplankton, and other small fish

Predators: bigger fish, crabs, and orca and humpback whales

Big Fish

Prey: small fish, zooplankton, crabs, shrimp, and urchins

Predators: sharks, dolphins, seals, sea lions, bears, orca whales, and humans

Crabs

Prey: kelp and other plants, small fish, worms, and decaying matter

Predators: humans, octopuses, big fish, snails, and other crabs

Seals
(Harbor Seals)

Prey: squid, octopuses, clams, shrimp, and fish

Predators: orca whales, polar bears, humans, and sharks

Humpback Whales

Prey: plankton and small fish

Predators: orca whales and humans

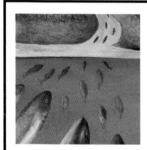

Salmon

Prey: plankton, fish, squid, and shrimp

Predators: humans, seals, orca whales, eagles, seabirds, bears, and sea lions

Humans

Prey: urchins, crabs, shrimp, fish, whales, and seals

Predators: none

Orca Whales

Prey: other whales, seals, sea lions, fish, sharks, birds, and sea turtles

Predators: none

Seasons Come and Go, Around and Around

Spring

On land, plants bud and blossom in the **spring**; in the ocean, marine plants bloom too. Just like land animals, many fish and marine animals are born or hatch in the spring when plants and food are plentiful. These births signal a time of feasting so important that humpback whales travel thousands of miles to dine on the newly hatched fish and blooms of plankton.

Summer

During the **summer**, insects swarm on land and marine plants (phytoplankton) and invertebrates float on the sea's surface. Near the shore, dense tangles of kelp and other seaweeds create undersea forests. Some small fish lay their eggs on these sea plants. Herring and other small forage fish swim away from the shore and become important food for whales.

Autumn

Autumn winds blow leaves from trees on land. In the ocean, powerful winds whip the waves that tear leaves and entire plants from the sea floor. Tangles of these plants float like small islands, offering birds, and even seals, a resting place at sea. The seaweed tangles also wash onto beaches, creating another important food source for small marine life.

Winter

Winter brings colder weather to land and the ocean. In some areas, rain turns to snow and ice might line the ocean shore. In other areas, it gets cold but not enough to snow. Some animals migrate or move to warmer areas in the winter. *What are some other animals that migrate? What are some other ways that animals protect themselves from the colder weather?*

Ocean Food Web

Our food comes from many sources. Most of us simply buy it at the grocery store without paying attention to where food is grown or prepared. Yet, some of us still catch fish from the sea, pick berries in the meadows, or visit local farms for fresh fruits and vegetables.

Imagine how different life is for wild animals. They never go to a grocery store or restaurant and don't get to come inside for hot chocolate on a cold, winter day! They have to find or catch their own food when and where it is available.

Plants are the "bottom" of food webs because they make their own food by getting their energy from the sun. Seaweed, kelp, eel, and turtle grass are all types of ocean plants. The most common ocean plants are called **phytoplankton**.

Zooplankton are tiny floating animals that eat phytoplankton. Some stay the same their entire lives. Others are early life stages of much larger animals such as lobsters, crabs, and other sea life.

Together, phytoplankton and zooplankton are just called **plankton**. Most are so tiny you would need a microscope to see each one. But they appear in such large numbers, that they often paint miles and miles of the sea with a solid wash of colorful plankton blooms.

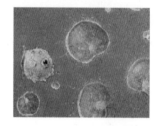

Some zooplankton, such as shrimp-like krill, can be two inches long and weigh a gram (about as much as a paper clip). While some plankton such as krill can swim a little, most drift with the wind and tides. Not only do smaller animals eat plankton, but the largest animals on earth eat plankton—blue whales!

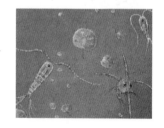

Baby animals live in shallow waters where **kelp forests**, **mangrove swamps**, and **salt marshes** make important **nursery habitats**. They can hide in the dense growth of plants, where there is lots of food to eat as plankton and chunks of plants swirl in with the tides.

When animals in the nurseries get bigger, many start swimming farther and farther in search of food, deeper waters, or distant breeding grounds.

Thanks to Dr. Thomas C. Eagle, Fishery Biologist, National Marine Fisheries Service, NOAA (DC)
and Rita Bell, Education Programs Manager at the Monterey Bay Aquarium
for verifying the accuracy of the information in this book.

Hirschi, Ron.
Ocean seasons / by Ron Hirschi ; illustrated by Kirsten Carlson.
    p. : col. ill. ; cm.

Includes "For Creative Minds" section with food web cards and information on how
seasonal changes affect ocean plants and animals.

ISBN: 978-0-97774-2325 hardcover
ISBN: 978-1-60718-8636 paperback
ISBN: 978-1-60718-0180 English eBook downloadable
ISBN: 978-1-934359-532 Spanish eBook downloadable
ISBN: 978-1-60718-2641 Interactive, read-aloud eBook featuring selectable English and Spanish text and
audio (web and iPad/tablet based)

1. Marine ecology--Juvenile literature. 2. Food chains (Ecology)--Juvenile literature. 3. Marine ecology.
4. Food chains (Ecology) I. Carlson, Kirsten M. (Kirsten Michelle), 1968- II. Title.

QH541.5.S3 H57 2007
577.7   2006924850

Manufactured in China, June 2013
This product conforms to CPSIA 2008
6th Printing

Sylvan Dell Publishing
Mt. Pleasant, SC 29464
www.SylvanDellPublishing.com